Training Simulation
- Trends & Issues -
Modeling & Simulation in Training

Employee Relations Training Exercise for Human Resource Professionals and Supervisory Managers

Dawn D. Boyer, Ph.D.

Book Copyright:	2017© by Dawn D. Boyer, Ph.D.
ISBN Numbers:	ISBN-13: 978-1-948149-00-6 ISBN-10: 1-948149-00-1
Copyright Notice:	2017©: The Author supports copyright. Copyright sparks creativity, encourages diverse viewpoints, and promotes free speech, and creates a vibrant and rich art culture. Thank you for buying an authorized copy of this copyrighted book and for complying with international copyright laws. All copyrights are reserved. No part of this book, including interior design, cover design, icons, and pictures, may be reproduced or transmitted in any form, by any means (electronic, photocopying, recording, or otherwise) without the prior written permission of the copyright owner. Independent of the author's economic rights, and even after the transfer of the said rights, the author shall have the right to claim authorship of the work and to object to any distortion, modification of, and/or other derogatory action in relation to the said work that could be deemed prejudicial to the author's honor or reputation. No part of this book or images – black and white, or other renditions of images, are to be posted to any social media, Internet, and/or other digital media or platforms without prior written permission of the copyright owner. You are supporting writers and allowing the author to continue to publish books for every other reader to continue to enjoy.
Trademarks:	All brand names, product names, logos, service marks, trademarks or registered trademarks are trademarks of their respective owners.

Author's Business Website	www.DBoyerConsulting.com
Amazon Author Page:	https://www.amazon.com/author/dawnboyer
Review Author's Books:	www.shelfari.com/DawnDeniseBoyer
Facebook Author's Page:	www.facebook.com/DawnBoyerAuthor
Facebook Business Page:	www.Facebook.com/DBoyerConsulting
Google+ Business Page:	https://plus.google.com/112802498128568560150/about?hl=en
LinkedIn	www.linkedin.com/in/DawnBoyer
Twitter:	www.Twitter.com/Dawn_Boyer

INTRODUCTION

This project was completed in the 2010 class of Old Dominion Universities' Occupational and Technical Studies in Educaton class, Issues in Training, Modeling and Simulation class. The assignment was to create a Simulation Lesson Design.

The following pages showase the assignment (proposal) for an instructional lesson that utilized simulation in support of a specific training or educational goal or objective. Using lectures in the classroom, assigned readings, and literature reviews, the following lesson plan was developed as the final project in the class.

Additionally, this book includes annotations and resources used by the student to gain more in-depth understanding of the principal and the project.

Simulation Proposal

Objectives:

Identify the subject of a simulation-based education or training project.

Develop preliminary elements of the simulation-based education or training project in sufficient detail so that it provides the framework that will guide solutions to close the gap in knowledge or skill.

Activity:

Develop a proposal for a training or educational lesson that utilizes simulation in support of a specific training or educational goal or objective.

Training Proposals

The training proposal will be for a lesson that utilizes a simulation, simulator, or virtual environment that either introduces trainees to new learning or allows experienced trainees to practice rare or critical situations not possible with traditional training methods. The proposal will represent a feasible training need and it should support a training solution to a training problem.

Education Proposals

The education proposal is a lesson that uses utilizes a simulation, simulator, or virtual environment that either introduces students to new learning or allows them to practice or experience situations through simulated methods. The lesson must represent the real world, and should support the school curriculum.

The Proposal

Prepare a proposal for a lesson that uses a simulation, simulator, or virtual environment (computer-based or non-computer-based). The activity requires significant research, thinking, and problem-solving. The learner was required to turn in a professional quality package that contains the following items:

- Proposed course or training module title
- Description of the instructional problem
- Course or training module description and justification
- Thorough description of the learner and/or target audience
- Description of the learning tasks to be covered
- Instructional objectives
- Justification for using simulation, simulator, or virtual environment
- Thorough description of the simulation, simulator, or virtual environment to be used:

- ✓ Description and type of simulation
- ✓ Scope of the simulation (The "breadth" -- in general terms, what basic concepts
- ✓ and skills will be covered)
- ✓ Links between learning objectives and simulation attributes
- ✓ Fidelity assessment linking attributes of the simulation and related activities to
- ✓ the learning objectives, learners, and tasks

- Framework required to support the simulation

  - ✓ Problem/Scenario
  - ✓ Participant roles
  - ✓ Staff and peripheral roles
  - ✓ Anticipated events
  - ✓ Projected sequence
  - ✓ Projected supplemental material
  - ✓ Consequences

- Resource Requirements

Review past proposals to gain an understanding of this project assignment and to document the choices made regarding the fidelity of the simulation or simulator chosen. Review the proposal to integrate suggestions and comments.

Product:

Course Information:

Course title & description
Course justification fits instructional problem & target audience

Simulation Information:

Type, scope, & description of the simulation
Proposed simulation fits instructional problem & target audience
Simulation fidelity justified & appropriate

Framework:

Learning objectives
Description of the scenario(s), roles (participant, staff, peripheral), events, & sequence
Anticipated supplemental materials

Overall:
Simulation plan is feasible & complete
Graduate-level grammar, spelling & formatting

TRAINING AND SIMULATION MODEL

HRP/Practitioner (HRP) Employee Relations

GENERAL GUIDE:

This easy to portage, DVD-CBT-based training assists human resource professionals (HRP) in preparing themselves psychologically, socially, mentally, and proactively to various scenarios, at multiple levels of dynamics, within any type of business or company environment. Most HRP's, as they advance into the lower, middle, and then upper levels of management and supervision have never had the opportunity to deal with employee relationship issues. Because many of these issues pivot around very emotional situations, it's best to get training on what "could" happen first before encountering something "would" happen. Additionally, in companies where there is no HRP, an experienced manager or supervisor may need to step up to the plate to resolve the concern. This training allows a 'glimpse' of the type of emotional issues which may result in conflict and provides reasonable and legal resolutions from which to pick and choose, based on the type of employee and relations issue.

Small company's employees may work in tight spaces, where there is little privacy, or the relationships may mix family, 'favorite' peers, and other unique co-worker situations, resulting in potential 'pressure-cooker' events. Whether there is a new 'outsider' coming into the environment, or an 'internal conflict' brewing, it's best to know how to deal with the potential event.

Bigger companies have large numbers of employees, where they really don't get to know many others outside the department, and may be put in environments where there is 'office politics' or simply no time to encourage better communications. Over the last few decades, more work is being squeezed out of fewer people, and the economy and company financial pressure are pushing employees to provide a greater ROI for their activities. Speed and technology cause confusion and reliance more on e-mails, electronic bulletin boards, company servers, fewer staff meetings, and web-based cloud computing, as well as telecommuting. This opens miscommunications to more occurrences.

To resolve those miscommunications, someone must step in and salve hurt feelings, track down and investigate occurrences that might cause the company legal liability, resolve issues on work spaces, communications, provide a shoulder to cry on, as well as documenting issues to ensure incidents are ready for explanation even after the main players may have moved on, in any audits demanded by government entities.

APPROACH:

Starting with simple, and easy to solve circumstances, the training modules will work through low-level, emotional-based scenarios involving interaction with actors playing the parts of company employees seeking an empathic ear and/or a solution to a personal problem, and work up to more complex incidences involving scenarios with more than one employee involved, but dealing with the unhappy employee who may be at one end or the other of a harassment issue, bullying, disciplinary action, etc.

The learner for these modules will sit at the computer, as if they were sitting at a desk in their office, and the actor/employees will come into the office (simulated on the computer screen), have a seat, and then learners will have several script choices which they will read out loud to practice what is 'best-case' scenario for the issue at hand (if known ahead of time), toggle a button that indicates this is their choice, and the employee will react appropriately to the logic chain. If the learner picks the incorrect scenario, the employee will negatively react, and the module will explain why the more correct answer would have been a better choice.

ROI:

Using this simple to use, CBT module allows HRP's to study, model and practice their actions and voice inflections, as well as learn from others who have already been through the scenarios in real-life situations how to best react, or not react, to employee relations within a business or work environment. This inexpensive training platform would allow this type of program to easily be implemented within any size company and budget.

TRAINING PROPOSAL

This training proposal is for a lesson-utilizing simulation, simulator, or virtual environment which either introduces trainees to new learning or allows experienced trainees to practice rare or critical situations not possible with traditional training methods or within the working environment with peers or co-workers because of the potential volatility. It will represent a feasible training need and supports a training solution to a training problem. This is original work, not something developed previously.

Simulation Section	Description of Simulation
Proposed course or training module title / description	**Employee Relations Training Exercise for Human Resources Practitioners**
Definitions / Abbreviations:	CBT – Computer Based Training EE - Employee HR – Human Resources HRP – HRPs (or Practitioners) SE – Simulated Employees
Description of the instructional problem	HRPs (HRP's) rarely have the 'real life' opportunity to practice reactions to employees' complaints, emotional outbursts, or ethical issues that crop up in day-to-day workplace environments. In many cases, HRP's may be

Simulation Section	Description of Simulation
Justification for instructional problem & target audience	surprised and respond in a personal versus professional manner to the situation.

This instructional simulation will provide various types of employee relation situations and guide the learner through practice of best case scenario, via professional behavior and responses. The simulation will attempt to portray a number of scenarios, and how to handle them, within a non-threatening learning environment to give a baseline of knowledge for proper and ethical behavior to resolve the situations.

While this course will be targeted to HRP's, it can also be marketed to companies who are too |

Simulation Section	Description of Simulation
	small for an HR manager or department, where supervising managers or the owner act in lieu of a 'HR' representative.
Course or training module description and justification	HRP's will go through a simulation where a 'simulated employee' will react to several levels of the following different situations: • termination for cause – disciplinary, lay-offs, failure to thrive, failure to return after medical leave/FMLA, etc. • ethical behavior problems – sexual harassment, work behavior, improper use of computer or electronic media, etc.

Simulation Section	Description of Simulation
	- emotional crisis handling – personal problems at home or work, inability to co-exist peacefully with co-workers, etc.
- employee inter-relational problems – EEOC or ADA issues, religion in the workplace, etc.
- personal behavioral problems - physical or mental issues, naiveté of proper etiquette, body language, communication issues, etc.
- threats of violence to self or peers – anger management, stalking, etc.

The learner will watch, analyze, review, and then |

Simulation Section	Description of Simulation
	respond via several choices provided in that unique model. They will 'learn through doing' on how to respond most appropriately (best practices) to emotional cues from the simulated employee (crying, anger, violence, etc.).
	The stability of the content, whether it is verbal or manipulative – requires decision making on the part of the learner and the difficulty of those decisions - determines to a great extent, the strategy most appropriate in real-life.
Description of the learner and/or target audience	HRP's who have reached a supervisory and/or management level must deal with employees in several states of

Simulation Section	Description of Simulation
Type, scope, & description of the simulation	emotions and must also deal with reactions from employees when unexpected situations arise.
Proposed simulation for instructional problem & target audience	The target audience are HRP's who have reached a level within their career where they are supervising employees within their department, but must also deal with employees of their company or organization who come to them to ask for assistance in dealing with unethical or personal problems, as well as issuing terminations, or notices of disciplinary actions. The secondary target are those who are supervisors in non-HR departments who are the first line of defense in

Simulation Section	Description of Simulation
	problem solving in dealing with employees on the line.
	Employees (EE's) are mostly predictable for reactions in any given situation, but in some cases may be totally unpredictable, and have actual or perceived violent behavior reactions. HRP's who have not dealt with such human behaviors before may be taken off guard, as well as take the behavior personally. This results in an unsatisfactory action or reaction for both the company and the employee in the situation.
	Modeling behaviors that are *best practice* for known employee relation specific situations in advance gives HRP's the opportunity to

Simulation Section	Description of Simulation
	practice, and react accordingly to the employee relation situation, as well as learn how to handle the reactions within a safe environment, when it occurs in real life situations.
	In this training simulation, the learners will actively talk 'to' the program, verbally out loud, as part of the instructional training, to listen to tone of voice as they speak, as well as learning to emphasize the most diplomatic words to tactfully communicate messages.
	For instance: An employee comes into the office crying and can't seem to stop during a conversation that is dealing with normal business

Simulation Section	Description of Simulation
	activities, and it's a repeat scenario – the employee does this all the time. The learner would have different choices to react: a) ignore the crying and continue to talk as if nothing was happening b) ask the employee if they wish to go home c) diplomatically and tactfully tell the employee they are excused to go to the bathroom, but once they've composed themselves, come straight back to the manager's office to finish the conversation

Simulation Section	Description of Simulation
	d) tell the employee it is obvious the job is too stressful; would they want to be considered for a lower stress position or would they need some time to start looking for a new job… The reasoning – the employee has learned that repeating this emotional scenario, allows her to escape some tasking, avoid communicating with those she doesn't wish to, and avoid having to perform to minimum expectations. The best answer to this question is (c) – let the employee compose themselves and come back to work, with no less expectations of

Simulation Section	Description of Simulation
	performance, and if it continues to repeat, then to got scenario (d).
	This simulation is based on HRP's needing private instruction on personality behavior of employees, and relies on HRP's having the ability and capability to perform CBT, as well as technological capability (high school or college level of education; PC capable; prior experience, education, or training in Human Resources; and the ability to read, write, and speak to employees in a one-on-one scenario). Performing via verbal responses, reacting to the behavior demonstrated on screen, and learning what the 'legal' as well as 'best-case'

Simulation Section	Description of Simulation
	scenarios options are, provide a better learning model for real-life practice.
Description of the learning tasks to be covered **Learning objectives**	This training will be designed as a CBT with human actors (who have been videotaped for each logic chain) portraying employees in various employee relations problem scenarios and situations, using the predominant emotional reactions of employees within a small- to large-size corporate or business environment. HRP's will review the situation in a written summary, and then view the Simulated Employee (SE) in a simulated office environment, as part of the video clip. It will look like

Simulation Section	Description of Simulation
	the employee is entering the office, in front of the learner, and sit down (or start acting the part), facing the HRP (they are facing the learner on the monitor). Scripts will appear at the bottom of the monitor screen, providing prompts, and descriptions. The learner may also pause the program to read a pop-up box for clues they may be missing. Then as the simulated employees speak, their words will come up on screen (for the hearing impaired learner), and the HRP will have a certain restricted time to react by reading the potential 'reactions' in script form at the bottom of the screen and clicking on the

Simulation Section	Description of Simulation
	best case scenario of their choice.
	The HRP's will 'read out loud' their role script, and the actors will react to the conversation, again – as part of a video clip.
	The second part will be the HRP's will have a choice of the 'read out loud' script for their reactions to what the simulated employee says. A logic branch of text at the bottom of the screen allows the learner to make their choice after reading out loud, and will take the HRP's decision choice through bad and/or good decisions and reactions in branching logic.
	The simulation responses overall will be based on timed default

Simulation Section	Description of Simulation
	reading times (allowing the learner time to read the reaction scripts, plus the timing of each scenario at the beginning of each module); plus time allowed for rapid and timely responses to the SE's verbal and visual clues during the training module. Each scenario can be accomplished within 15 – 20 minutes, and can be picked independently to enable module choices on which to train within the complete package.

The goal is to choose modules in succeeding order of ease for resolving up to hard to resolve, for best impact of and use of scenario modeling and learning. At the end of each |

Simulation Section	Description of Simulation
	module, a written description (which could also be verbalized by the computer so learner can listen instead) of the scenario, what generalized steps were taken, why they were taken, and what the best case results were because of these steps will formally summarize the learning. To provide a formative assessment, each module could have a 'test' situation, that is parallel to the module just completed, the learner can go through without prompting or pop-up boxes, to see if they learned enough to be able to solve this employee relationship issue without assistance.

Simulation Section	Description of Simulation
Instructional objectives	Simply put, the instructional objectives are:
	1. Review scenario to prepare the learner
	2. Apply the script – allow the learner to grasp a comfort level following the logical step-by-step procedure to resolve an employee issue
o Audience	3. Recognize and identify situations via body language, verbalization, and other communication methods
o Learned Behavior Goals	4. Choose the most appropriate or best-practice response to resolve the issue without harm to the employee, or at best

Simulation Section	Description of Simulation
	case, with the least amount of negative impact 5. Learn to apply what is learned to parallel and/or similar but different scenarios
o Goal One	The audience for this simulation is HRP's who have reached a supervisory and/or management level must deal with employees in varying states of emotions when expected or unexpected situations arise. Additionally, supervisory managers can use these to learn the 'first line of defense' to solve the employee relations issues before they need to reach the human resources department.

Simulation Section	Description of Simulation
o Goal Two	*Knowledge: The learners should be able to identify when an employee relation issue arises, which warrants HR involvement; and be able to comprehend when it warrants a private consultation.*
	Psychomotor: The learners should be able to be ready to react mentally or physically, based on the scenario presented.
o Goal Three	*Affective: The learners will demonstrate what information is best to gather to be able to act according to the scenario.*
	At the end of each simulation, the learners will be able to demonstrate the

Simulation Section	Description of Simulation
	proper responses to employee relations in imaginary scenarios based on real-life environment and situations.
	Knowledge: The learners should be able to apply learned and general methods of dealing with the situation to each specific situation – whether as a counseling or as an employment action.
	Psychomotor: The learners will learn to guide the scenario, using verbal and physical actions and responses. Learners should also be aware of uncontrollable psychomotor signs that would or could make the

Simulation Section	Description of Simulation
	scenario better or worse.

Affective: The learners will demonstrate how to respond (physically and mentally) by listening, formulating a response, and presenting the response in a diplomatic and nonthreatening manner.

The learners will be able to demonstrate (emulate) the ability to discuss employee relations situations and problems directly with 'real-life' employees based on learning demonstrated within the simulation.

Knowledge: The learners will demonstrate the ability to apply learned, |

Simulation Section	Description of Simulation
	general methods to comprehend the circumstances leading up to the employee relations situation and the prescribed actions required to solve / resolve the issue, and/or prevent further reoccurrence.
	Psychomotor: The learners will demonstrate the ability to verbally have a conversation, guide the direction of the conversation, while mentally tracking the physical elements of the scenario.
	Affective: The learners will demonstrate how to respond to a new scenario by building

Simulation Section	Description of Simulation
	upon learned responses from previous scenarios.
	The learners will be able to demonstrate the proper response to employees for most case scenarios in real-life.
	Knowledge: The learners will be able to apply learned and general comprehension of the circumstances leading up to the employee relations situation, as well as actions required to prevent further escalation.
	Psychomotor: The learners will demonstrate the use of physical cues and verbal language to modify, disarm,

Simulation Section	Description of Simulation
	physically change the behavior or mentally change the attitude of persons within the scenario.
	Affective: The learners will demonstrate how to respond to a new scenario by building upon learned responses from previous scenarios within the training program.
Instructional objectives o to introduce a subject o to provide remedial assistance	This simulation uses demonstration, simulation, performance, programmed instruction, and pre-study as a combination of basic approaches. The objective(s) for this simulation is to provide supporting and alternative approaches to appropriate,

Simulation Section	Description of Simulation
o to accelerate, enrich, or build business skills o to teach verbal and cognitive decision skills o to build upon concepts o to improve reasoning problem-solving ability	ethical, and best practice behavioral guidelines to HRP's responsible for resolving employee relations concerns for employers and organizations. HRP's will learn initially through private practice of the methodology, best behaviors in given (common) situation(s): what not to say, what to say, how to act or react, so situations result in a best case or positive solution to the employee relationship problem, issue, or concern. HRP's will demonstrate the ability to understand, empathize, and sympathize with employees who are facing dilemmas and/or who need to make difficult

Simulation Section	Description of Simulation
	personal decisions based on work-related and unexpected situations, so the HRP may assist and guide the employees in making decisions that will benefit them, and avoid any legal or liability related costs in the long-run.
Justification for using simulation, simulator, or virtual environment **Simulation fidelity justification & appropriateness**	Human emotions are volatile. It is best to practice handling professional business environment reactions to emotional or potentially explosive situations within a 'green zone' (no penalty) and privately, so learners can best learn how to react appropriately. This allows practice for the best use of words and language to calm the employee and the

Simulation Section	Description of Simulation
	situation down to a level with which the learner is comfortable, and can make the employee comfortable, before pushing the HRP moves to a higher fidelity situation with live actors or into real-life.
	There is no best method of teaching this type of scenario which is applicable to the learning situations and instructional objectives of this module. This entry-level simulation strategy is compatible with objectives of the instruction, the nature of the training, facilities and equipment available, and the educational or career background, and business environment level of the trainees. Most HRP's or managers have their offices

Simulation Section	Description of Simulation
	at work or use of a computer at home where they can use the learning modules to practice in privacy. Additionally, this can be used in small, intimate groups of 2-4 HRP's or managers, where the CBT can be paused while short group discussions occur for the best decision, as well as round-robin verbalization for each group member so each can practice, and use team commentary on voice inflection or mannerisms to add to the fidelity of the learned behavior for the exercise. The methodology for these scenarios also includes verbal communication and

Simulation Section	Description of Simulation
	cognitive decision making, as well as practicing responses and response speed within scenarios.
Description of simulation, simulator, or virtual environment used: o Description and type of simulation	This simulation instructional technique complements the handling of visual and auditory responses via visual and auditory aids. Using CBT (PowerPoint or other instructional software modeling for simulations) used as a technology device to model a trainee response system (with pre-recorded videos) is one that is somewhat cost effective. The HRP learner sits at a computer and guides themselves through multiple scenarios of employee relationship

Simulation Section	Description of Simulation
	issues. Learners 'talk to' the SE's (computer) by reading the screen scripts aloud from the choices they make for what they believe is best practice logic branch. SE actors will talk to the HRP (learner) directly, as if they were sitting at a desk in an office environment.
o Scope of the simulation (The "breadth" -- in general terms, what basic concepts and skills will be covered)	Media include printed materials and graphics in the form of video and sound recordings on DVDs.
o Links between learning objectives and simulation attributes	Additionally, responses will be timed. Learners will be given a default time-out for reading the various responses, but if a decision is not made with X seconds after reading through the logic chain, then brownie points will be deducted for not deciding in a timely

Simulation Section	Description of Simulation
o Fidelity assessment linking attributes of the simulation and related activities to the learning objectives, learners, and tasks	manner how to best react to the SE's script or scenario actions. Learners can also use the pop-up boxes for further explanation for the decisions they make, and why or why not their decisions work best for the scenario. This capability allows for instant formative assessment throughout the modules to avoid training by the learner in the 'wrong' even reinforcing, negative behavior. The scope of the simulation is to present various situations acted out by SE's to cover between four to six scenarios most likely to occur as a employee relations issue within a working business environment. The skills to

Simulation Section	Description of Simulation
	be covered are communications resolving or solving employee issues ranging from: 1) not getting along with a peer, 2) termination for cause, 3) emotional employee unable to perform due to personal or office relationships or issues, 4) a dangerous employee threatening safety and security to peers and coworkers, etc., to name a few. Basic skills taught will be how best to speak to the Simulated Employee; how to react to negative or potentially violent emotions; SE's will react suddenly or unexpectedly so HRP's will be 'surprised' (often) at the emotional reaction, which would model potential 'real-

Simulation Section	Description of Simulation
	life' situations; and how best to handle specific situations given the emotional state of the SE's. The learner will encounter an employee pulling out a gun and waving it around, an inconsolable crier, an employee who has been a victim of sexual harassment, etc. When the employees enter the HRP's office, they may seem normal, but the instant their behavior changes, the HRP should be aware of how to act or not to act, to avoid harm or negative consequences.

To avoid any mental or physical, and potential harm to new learners in watching these surprise scenarios, they will be warned ahead |

Simulation Section	Description of Simulation
	of the module (pop up letters on screen) that this module contains surprising elements, and to be prepared.[1]

The learning objectives are to expose the HRP's to real-life situations which they may encounter during their career; prepare them for the 'sudden' onset or occurrence of these potentially volatile situations, to be prepared to handle those employee relation issues with appropriate reactions, communications, and to ensure the situations are resolved appropriately, ethically, sympathetically, |

---

[1] *In some cases, the learners themselves may be survivors of work-related employee relations issues. To avoid any PTSD episodes heart attacks, or other life-threatening negative reactions, a warning will let them know something is coming, to mentally prepare for that 'surprise' element, without giving away the show, per se.*

Simulation Section	Description of Simulation
	and positively for all involved. The simulation value is most HRP's may never have an opportunity to practice this type of scenario before a real event, the surprise may take them off-guard, and may result in inappropriate and personalized behavior.

The fidelity of the scenario is low-to-moderate in this simulation, mostly because HRP's need to be slowly immersed into these types of potentially volatile activities, but not feel so threatened initially they become too frightened to handle the situation if it does occur in real life. This low-to-moderate fidelity will give them the exposure, but not physically put them in |

Simulation Section	Description of Simulation
	the scenario or real danger; while concentrating on teaching the learners proper, ethical, and professional behavioral reactions, while not having to stress about reacting to 'real people.'
Framework required to support the simulation: o Problem/Scenario o Participant roles	The problem scenario will take place (via CBT) as if the learner is sitting behind their office desk, and the SE's come into the office either: 1) because they were called in so HR could discuss or present an issue, or 2) because the employee sought the help of HR in resolving an problem. Participant roles are of a responsive HRP (the learner) currently in a

Simulation Section	Description of Simulation
o Staff and peripheral roles o Anticipated events o Projected sequence o Projected supplemental material	career track or who is in the supervisory position for employee relations. The HRP's are expected to resolve employee relations issues in a best practice manner that resolves the concerns to avoid liability, but gain employee trust, or bring the matter to a conclusion without harm to the employee or the company. SE's act out the parts of the employee's with the problems to be resolved. Simulated (actor) Employees will speak directly to the computer screen (video-taped) with scripted lines, portraying the characteristics of an employee with an assigned employee relation issue.

Simulation Section	Description of Simulation
o Consequences Simulation plan = feasible & complete	There are no peripheral roles in play for this simulation. In initial cases, the scenario will be expected, and HRP's will develop a comfort zone for reactions and problem solving. Later scenario's will surprise the HRP – SE's will turn violent or threaten the HRP, jump toward the screen (in the learner's face), and act as if threatening the learner physically. The HRP will have various choices of reactions on the screen, asked to make a decision to react in an appropriate manner to: 1) avoid personal injury, or the employee from harming themselves, or 2) to react

Simulation Section	Description of Simulation
	in a way that calms the employee down to a resolution of the problem.
	The sequence will be starting the learner with mild employee issues initially, and then work up to the more volatile situations – such as an employee threatening violence to peers or co-workers as a result of getting terminated.
	The course comes with a guidebook, as well as pre-test materials, that get the learner to thinking ahead of time what should be done in any scenario's circumstances. Additionally, formative assessments throughout the exercise strengthen learning, while post-test

Simulation Section	Description of Simulation
	materials will assess if the learner absorbed the understanding of behavioral goals. The guidebook will cover most, if not all, of the material in the proposal, explanations for, reasons why, where the 'best-case' scenario solutions came from, how to best handle employees in office layouts (HRP near the door for violent employees), a written script for all the scenarios so HRP's can go back, if needed later, for a quickie reference.
	The consequences of the simulation is learners (HRP's or Supervisory Managers) have a baseline of understanding of what best to do in scenarios

Simulation Section	Description of Simulation
	involving employees and employee relationship issues. They have practiced reacting to those scenarios in a safe environment thus have started to intrinsically incorporate ideas of behavior, as well as understanding the emotional viewpoint of the employee's in these situations.
Resource Requirements	The requirements for using this simulation are computer access and basic technology understanding. Video clip presentations of Simulated Employees will provide the multiple scenarios for reactive responses from the learner. A reference manual with

Simulation Section	Description of Simulation
	scenarios described will provide additional explanation for referencing.
	Additionally, for those learners who are hearing handicapped, a manual is provided which enables them to pick and choose scenarios manually through branching logic, as well as descriptive terms used for SE clips to describe the emotions and volatility of the scenario. They will be able to view the video, read the SE verbal responses with text clues to interpret the mannerisms, and be able to make valid and subjective responses based on this method. Timing can be turned off for hearing disabled to allow them time to read through the

Simulation Section	Description of Simulation
	materials versus respond within timing defaults.
Evaluation/Assessment	This scenario modeler will provide a CBT pre-test to see how learners would react to any given scenario; then put them through the scenario (multiple) with formative assessments at the end of each training module; as well as a post-test to ascertain if the simulation provided them enough effective guidance and training to improve upon their previously noted reactions to any given scenario.

ANNOTATIONS AND JOURNAL REVIEWS IN PREPARATION FOR DESIGNING MODELING & SIMULATION TRAINING MODEL

ANNOTATED BIBLIOGRAPHY AND JOURNAL ARTICLES ON PREPARATION OF TRAINING AND DEVELOPING A SIMULATION TRAINING MODEL

Games and Simulations: A New Approach in Education?

Computers have been around over 30 years, and games designed and played on computers have been around over twenty-nine point nine years. In the three years since this article was published, the advanced in technology has exponentially grown in comparison to the previous three years to the articles writing. Computer has become so linked to training and development via the use of games, simulations, modeling, and educational environments it is expected. In the mid-80's, while earning my Masters, I had to visit the university library (hoping they wouldn't close in the evenings before I was able to grab and copy a few articles for my research), meticulously look the articles up in bound journals, the Dewey Decimal catalog card drawers, or walk up and down seemingly miles of magazine stacks and read indexes of articles to determine articles I wanted to include. Today, grabbing and downloading an article is simply a matter of getting on the Internet, signing into my school library, querying on a few key words, and I'm provided more articles than I can review in years, much less a lifetime.

A hundred years ago pilots learned to fly planes by seat-of-the-pants, hands-on learning, and while airplanes weren't quite as expensive as they are today, many planes did go down from inexperienced pilots who were not trained sufficiently. Today's large airplanes are flown by commercial airline pilots[2] who must put in thousands of hours. Military jet fighter pilots must use jet fighter simulators to train on – the military can't afford to train a newbie on a million-dollar plane.

Primarily modeling and simulation games are used to provide experiential training situations, where rules are established, 'real life' situations are encountered, there may be some competitive elements, and have goals to increase or strengthen skill sets for the learner. The biggest complaint by learners might be that the games are 'not fun.'

---

[2] *This highest pilot certificate allows you to be the pilot in command (the captain) of a large commercial aircraft. It requires that you pass a written test, have a first-class medical certificate, are a high school graduate and have logged 1,500 flight hours including 250 hours as the pilot in command. Retrieved from:*
http://science.howstuffworks.com/pilot2.htm

But – have learners opened their eyes to the toy section at the local "Toys 'R Us?" There are rows of games that are educationally based simulation and modeling learning lessons. Learn to read, electronic pets (learn to take care of fake animal before a real animal), Excalibur Einstein Wizard (educational learning electronic games), electronic See and Say (learn to read for toddlers) are on a few of the thousands of simulation toys on the market. And, I've seen some adults get into the games more than the kids.

I like the statement the author quoted:

> "It may be argued that the relative ineffectiveness of instructional technology thus far has been caused by the application of the same old methods in new educational media—"New wine was poured, but only into old bottles" (Cohen & Ball, 1990, p. 334)"

I would venture to guess that many of the instructional methods that teachers use are those who are relatively new to the field, have been taught by others who were relatively 'new' to the field, and the same old standards of teaching technology simply gets passed along from teacher to teacher. Many may not have had newer and more exciting methods presented to them or they simply may not have the technological skill, background, or even the time, to make a more complex modeling and simulation, teaching module for their learners.

I have to argue with the author's statement about using games as a relatively new teaching style. My mother was a teacher between the mid-50's and late 60's and remember her putting together games for her elementary school students to play to learn their topic matter faster and better. I enjoyed practicing on her games while she ensured they worked. This was during a period (or era) of teaching where rote learning was the primary methodology of teaching students in primary grades.

The author did present three questions in this article that was somewhat philosophical, and a colloquia might be an interesting arena in which to discuss the possible answers. He presented his opinions and resources from which he provided the answers, but it would be interesting to have others debate the questions in an open forum.

1. What are games and simulations? What makes something a game or simulation? What are their educational uses? Do they really have an effect on learning?

2. What is happening in the instructional design/development (IDD) field? Is there a place for games and simulations in both the theory and the practices of IDD?

3. If games and simulations are useful educational tools, how can they be used in education? How can instructional designers take them into account, while designing learning environments? Are there any instructional design / development models (IDDMs) that would light up an instructional designer's path, guiding their journey to integrate games and simulations into their designs? (Akilli, 2007, p. 3).

Akilli notes there is a shift towards multiple Instructional Development Models, but they all seem to be similar, and the one thing that is striking in general is that there seems to be a shift from standardization to a customization of each model that focuses on individual or unique learning situations that are critically built around the learner, the subject matter, and the instructor's knowledge and Subject

Matter Expert (SME) skill sets. Additionally, there must be more than one solution to each logic chain or branch – because there are so many 'fuzzy' possibilities resulting from 'real-life' situations.

Citations/Bibliography

Akilli, G.K. (2007). Games and Simulations: A New Approach in Education. D. Gibson, C. Aldrich, M. Prensky (eds.) *Games and Simulations in Online Learning.* Hershey, London, Melbourne: Information Science Publishing, 1–20.

Developing a Teaching Portfolio: Seven Dimensions of Documenting a Teaching Portfolio

This was an interesting article because it seems that I've been doing this as rote during my tenure as a Human Resources manager as well as in past career stints as an instructor and teacher. I save everything! OK, I'm a self-professed pack-rat – but especially training courses I have taken online, handouts provided by presenters in symposiums, conferences, and small group presentations, everything is sacred to me as a learner. In the back of my mind, I keep thinking, this is good enough to use later if I ever have to teach or present on this subject. I have three foot stacks of stuff I need to get filed in my bedroom (my husband is going to kill me one day!) of articles, magazines, printed hand-outs, etc., that I'm saving for use in my PhD dissertation, my HR consulting business, and possibly for future teaching resources.

I understand keeping a portfolio of teaching materials, is akin to the documentation required for Capability Maturity Model Integration (CMMI) certification or ISO 9000 and ISO 14000 for Quality Assurance Models (Total Quality Management) for performance, manufacturing, processes, and policies. You record what worked, what worked best or better, how you taught specific subjects, what your students felt about the manner in which you taught, and other related documentation.

How does this relate to Modeling & Simulation in Education? Quite closely, as using a portfolio of methodologies that have worked (or will work based on similar or parallel teaching projects) in the past may be applied to the modeling for learning and outcome to which the instructor is aiming to reach for teaching the subject matter. Toward the end of the article, this is a list of documents and artifacts the author suggested instructors collect as part of their teaching portfolio.

The author suggested a portfolio include teaching documents such as: syllabi, schedules, assignments, lesson plans, lecture notes, review sheets, study guides, quizzes and tests, reading lists, bibliographies, and handouts. Instructional materials suggested in the portfolio are: PowerPoint Presentations, charts, project requirements, course contracts, concept maps, computer software, specification tables, simulations, case studies, outlines and materials, for demonstration, and any videos / films (modern version = YouTube URL links). Instructors should also collect student related documents such as: papers, projects, course grade profiles, photographs, performance videos, during-course feedback, audio recordings, test profiles, and end-of-course evaluations. As an instructor, any materials produced from the course should also be kept in the documentation form of publications, research, and subject matter monographs.

These types of materials would be very useful for future instructors to use for identical classes bringing in simulation and modeling techniques, and upon which more modern instructional methodology can be built. One example is the recent Introduction to Statistics class I took last fall. The course was horribly constructed as an asynchronous course (personal opinion). The instructor gave 'brownie points' for comments and constructive critiques each student parlayed forward to improve future classes. Because this class relied partially on Camtasia presentations from the instructor, the class units could be further developed into simulations of modules where the instructor runs through the finite steps of each statistical calculation for the students, as well as answering the general inquiry questions that occurred during the previous class(es).

Citations / Bibliography

Urbach, F. (1992, Spring). Developing a teaching portfolio: seven dimensions of documenting a teaching portfolio. *College Teaching*, 40(2), 71-74.

The Power of in-class Debates

I just finished compiling a presentation for another class for the definition of a teaching/learning style called colloquia, and one of the samples where it was used effectively was in university law classes where future juris doctorates were learning how to successfully debate within the courtroom. This methodology of using debate, according to this article, goes back further than Socrates and his teachings of philosophy, but further back to circa 481-411BC to Protagorus, who is considered the father of debate (think protagonist). According to this article, students retain and learn more effectively by analyzing, discussing, and using the results of the discussions in meaningful outcomes by applying the learning to situations by engagement. This method seemed to be even more advantageous for those with lower SAT scores to increase their critical thinking by active engagement.

Because true learning engages all the senses, using (or forcing) verbal and auditory skills to increase communication skills, and debates and open discussions will allow students to learn from each other, model proper verbal communication skills, and open their mind to others' opinions and viewpoints. Because debaters must be informed of their subject matter, they had to do research on the topic, then present and be prepared to debate the pros and cons (antagonist versus protagonist) of the viewpoint assigned.

The study focused on public speaking and debate before a group and the participants rating of their initial feelings before the first debate, then focusing more on the knowledge gained with subsequent debates, at the end of the study, the conclusion for a significant majority of the learners was that they learned 'a lot' from the exercise.

How can this method of debate prepare or be used in Modeling and Simulation? Already mentioned was the law students who used debate to prepare for courtroom appearances. Another use for debate within a Modeling and Simulation training would be ethics for business, personal, or religious models where results of a question would result in branching options, discussions, or results leading to a correct answer or multiple positive options.

Citations / Bibliography

Kennedy, R. R. (2009). The Power of in-class debates. *Active Learning in Higher Education*, 10, 225-236.

What Makes a Modeling and Simulation Professional?

This article is 13 years old, but it was interesting to go back that far to see how Simulation and Modeling careerists were defined in that period of time when computers were just becoming a major factor in everyday ordinary lives. This panel discussion came up with attributes or elements that a Modeling and Simulation professional would have: Attributes (specific to the job skills) related to a Systems Approach using the scientific method, People Skills related to Human Factors, Basic Skills related to discipline such as math, probability, research, management, physical science, and cost modeling & engineering to name a few, and Domain Knowledge of Modeling and Simulation methods including algorithms, software, programming languages, reductionism, and knowledge of and ability to use the Principle of Ockham's Razor (KISS) for design experimentation.

What is really interesting in this consensus paper is that even though it was written 13 years ago, all the relevant notes about what makes up a modeling and simulation professional are still true. In addition to the general skills and knowledge noted above, the author also mentioned additional knowledge needed – new technology software, data filtering and data-mining, engineering, operations research, training, human factors and ergonomics, artificial intelligence, visualization, sensory methodology, human behavior, and multiple disciplines and arenas of knowledge where parallel and inference can be exchanged within those domains. Today these skills sets are all still vital as part of the Knowledge, Strength, Integrity (KSI) requirements for modern day practitioners of modeling and simulation.

Citations / Bibliography

Rogers, R. (1997). ed. S. Andradóttir, K. J. Healy, D. H. Withers, and B. L. Nelson, What Makes a modeling and simulation professional?: the consensus view from one workshop. *Proceedings of the Winter simulation conference* (pp. 1375-1382). Orlando: University of Central Florida, P.O. Box 2500, Orlando, FL 32816, USA.

Simulations and games: Overcoming the barriers to their use in higher education

This article covered what the author believed to be the three main obstacles to using (modeling) simulation and games in higher institutions of learning: 1) suitability, 2) risks, and 3) resources. They classified the three main types of simulation-learning as role-playing, gaming, and computer stimulation.

In covering the suitability issue, the authors noted the games may not accurately portray real-world situations, may be too complex which would affect fidelity, and too much information may overwhelm the learners', and may also be over the students' heads for experience (either material, topic matter, or level of gaming).

Resources are always in critical demand in educational institutions. The simulation may cost more than the teacher, trainer, or department budget can fund, there may be a need for multiple administrative staff to support the simulation (again, man-hours cost money), and the most vital issue for resources is the 'time' available to the trainer to develop, the administrative staff to support, as well as the students ability to complete the training module.

The risks associated with gaming and simulation are student resistance (they don't like games), technical problems (computers, electronics), loss of control by the teacher, and a potential for a greater degree of control by the teacher for the learning experience, which reduces the flexibility of the students learning experience.

After research via interviews, the authors recognized strong links between the three barriers of risk, suitability, and resources and the constituent parts and how they interrelated to each other. Suitability components were: 1) availability, 2) learning outcomes, and 3) the type of student; Resource components were: 1) tangible, 2) intangible, and 3) time; while Risk components were: 1) lack of control, 2) technical problems, 3) student reactions, and 4) opportunity costs. The interview data resulted in highlighting the barriers, factors, and inter-relationships, but the authors noted the strongest were between suitability and resource.

The authors also provided some suggestions to get past the barriers for the three constraints to the simulation and gaming in the learning environment. A suggestion to overcome the time issue was for universities to designate a number of hours the instructor was to delegate specifically to development of training. Another suggestion was that training and development be provided more to instructors so they would know how to do gaming and simulation or how to develop this methodology for their course materials in the form of symposia, university-wide events, or pedagogic seminars. Another solution was the availability of software dedicated to creating gaming and simulations, funding for attending conferences and workshops, and libraries of learning resources. Two external organizations suggested for sources were the Higher Education Academy (HEA) Subject Centers and the Society for the Advancement of

Simulation and Gaming in Education and Training (SAGSET).

In conclusion, the authors addressed that these three barriers should be identified for higher institution of learning teaching staff by higher-ups with control of scheduling and budgets to increase the instructors' use of simulation and gaming in the classroom.

I did learn a new acronym from this article for future reference: simulations, games, and role-play (SGRP).

Citations / Bibliography

Moizer, ?, Lean, J., Towler, M., & Abbey, C. (2009). Simulations and games: overcoming the barriers to their use in higher education. *Active Learning in Higher Education*, 10, 207-224.

Active Involvement: Simulation Games and Teaching

Maria Montessori is the most likely early educator to take into consideration that children learn while playing games, and designed an early childhood curriculum around that principle of game simulation as a methodology to learning. Even today, children mimic their parents or other role models as they play games – playing house, mommy and daddy, driving the car, etc. Early childhood game simulation assist in learning early social development skills, but developing social skills is not the only use for 'fun' games. There are seven advantages of learning via gaming: 1) active student involvement, 2) gaming provides a high degree of enthusiasm; 3) abstract concepts are set in easier to understand scenarios, 4) there is immediate feedback to learners, 5) learners can experiment without feeling constant need to be correct, 6) learners can evaluate their own mistakes, and 7) communication skills are practiced (Maxson, 1973).

Sometimes the learning 'sticks' longer with those learners who obtained the knowledge via playing a game versus being taught in the traditional methodology. Additionally, the author noted that simulation and gaming instruction tended to show that learning retention rates were much higher, and when teachers are able to develop (or revise) their own simulation training they were able to pick more precise subject matter (topics), they were able to adjust the training to the students needs within their class (with whom they were familiar for abilities levels), and time constraints were not as strict because teachers could adjust the training as the game proceeded.

There were words of advice for facilitators of the teacher-led simulation gaming which were noted as four rules: 1) be concise, and only talk when necessary, 2) run the simulation game, don't try to control the learners, 3) be a game facilitator – not a leader or teacher, and 4) let the learners behave how they want to act or react. But overall, classroom management is vital to presenting a good gaming simulation.

Citations / Bibliography

Henson, K. (1982) Active Involvement: Simulation Games and Teaching, *NASSP Bulletin,* 66(454), 94-98

Jet Fighter: An Experiential Value Chain Exercise

Value chaining was first introduced in the 1985 book, *Competitive Advantage*, and widely taught to business students, management practitioners, and cited by academics in the area of strategic management, and is still used today in multiple areas and industries. Value chain is similar to ISO or quality assurance in that its meaning is related to citation and documentation text in management fields such as strategic management, accounting, entrepreneurship, information systems, logistics, economic development, health care (administration), and marketing efforts.

This exercise was developed as a game simulation to provide an opportunity for learners to understand an abstract concept (of value chain) and to use the elements of and to perform the various production steps of the activity. This exercise was an adaptation of another simulation exercise, but developed with a different learning objective. The exercise runs about two or more hours, and the objectives were to: 1) develop learner's ability to come up with tactics (ideas) to reduce cost/increase revenue using the concept of value chain analysis, 2) understand the positives and negatives of the process, and to understand when it is more appropriate to use the process. This exercise not only teaches about the concept, but also uses social interaction to serve as an ice-breaker.

The remainder of the article literally outlines the exercise, provides the steps and outcomes and discussions for the simulation and noted the types of learning that took place during the exercise as it related to value chaining. The authors' summarized how the students assessed and rated the exercise at the end of the article. This was an interesting piece about an actual gaming simulation that was able to be paralleled to real life situations by the learners once they understood the concept of the exercise.

Citations / Bibliography

Sheehan, N., Gamble, E. (2010, January), Jet Fighter: An Experiential Value Chain Exercise, *Journal of Management Education, XX(X)*, 1-25

Developing The Great Eight Competencies with Leaderless Group Discussion

Bartram, Robertson, and Callinan compiled a list of 112 competencies, then clustered those competencies to eight clusters, which they called the Great Eight competencies of work performance. These clusters were primarily: 1) leading and deciding, 2) supporting and cooperating, 3) interacting and presenting, 4) analyzing and interpreting, 5) creating and conceptualizing, 6) adapting and coping, 7) organization and execution, and 8) enterprising and performance. Corporate recruiters, in a Wall Street Journal survey, rated communication and interpersonal skills, team skills, and analytical problem solving as vital skill sets when seeking Master of Business Art candidates for positions. Result driven and leadership potential were rated just behind the first three sets of competencies. The question is – how can business educators develop these competencies within an educational setting for management students to prepare them for meeting these skills demands once they reach the 'real world?'

A methodology of Leaderless Group Discussion (LGD) was suggested by the author as a good training practice and concentrated the rationale for the method in this article. In order to develop a 'leadership' attitude, the students essentially needed to take on the leaderless group, which demands rapid decision-making and behavior that is inherent in the management level of business and corporations. Being able to exhibit "decisive behavior" is the heart of being able to demonstrate and illustrate the other cluster behaviors of the Great Eight.

Past forms of this exercise provides a 'problem' to a group of 6-8 students, while there are observers who act as assessors, and uses standard tools such as in-basket, oral presentations and writing assignments, interviews, testing (formal and formative), that work with the assessors in a program to identify those learners who may exhibit the potential for promotability. When this method was brought to the university setting, the students performed better in LGD rating scales than did those who were involved in the exercise methodology in corporate settings, and was an excellent predictor of future career success. Thus the recommendation was to use this method more actively in school environments.

The authors did note that the fidelity of the exercise was a possibly slightly less than real-life because of the access to real-world problems by the students, but the students did learn the disciplines, theories, concepts, and best-practices of business. The exercise provided 'model behavior' to the students, on which they could further develop the Great Eight competencies for real-world experience.

The objectives of the exercise in a educational setting are for students to develop a better understanding of organizational development, communication skills, and human resources management with the goal for the learners to have an improved cognitive understanding of middle- and upper-management roles within an organization. In short, they learned how to handle problems, make decisions, understand law, MC a business meeting, facilitate problem solving between peers, deliver an oral presentation, and learn specifics about business management. This article covered the steps in the exercise and what results were the goals.

The article did bring in the interesting concept of scores based on introverts versus extroverts, but was unable to pinpoint a research based confirmed assumption. The exercise was noted to have other shortcomings relative to the number of participants in the group, limited to one professor for oversight of the exercise, and the need for a business SME in management.

Citations / Bibliography

Costigan, R., Donahue, L. (2008, May), Developing the great eight competencies with leaderless group discussion, *Journal of Management Education, 33(5)*, 596-617

Individuality, Individual Differences, and Computer Simulation

I learned two new words in this article – nomothetic[3] and idiographic[4], which are approaches to the study of individual differences and individuality[5]. Although the author wrote this article in 1976, it's interesting how he noted the methodology for computer simulation hasn't really been explored to it's fullest extent yet and he could not understand why computers haven't been used to their fullest extent of technology and knowledge to offer very promising techniques in dealing with human behavior.

The theory was there is eight different perspectives for studying human behavior, similar to a 3-D block that looks like a Rubic's cube, but with four blocks versus nine blocks in the image. The

---

[3] *Psychology. pertaining to or involving the study or formulation of general or universal laws (opposed to idiographic).*
[4] *Psychology. pertaining to or involving the study or explication of individual cases or events (opposed to nomothetic).*
[5] *Terms introduced by Windelband in 1904 to distinguish the two sciences seeking general laws and structural patterns*

intersections of the blocks are: 1) number of individuals (one or many), 2) explanatory levels (functional or structural), and 3) Temporal Foci (state [static, enduring] or dynamic properties). This hypercube provides the dimensions of conceptual perspectives, and the author suggested that these concepts are not present in computer simulations at the writing.

This article most likely parallels the theory that computer simulations are not being used as they could be used – even today – with the technology available to teachers and facilitators of learning in work or educational environments. Although computers were not as available and affordable in 1976 as they are now, the cost effectiveness or ROI on developing sims today are just as serious an expense as they were in that time period.

Citations / Bibliography

Kearsley, G. (1976, May), Individuality, individual differences, and computer simulation, *Educational and Psychological Measurement, 36,* 811-823

Gaining A Perspective on Simulation and Gaming

It's interesting to read over 'older' journal articles as researchers discuss simulation and gaming, and it's clear that simulation, gaming, and this educational methodology is not a new type of training. This article is from 1973 (while I was still in high school) while another article I read was printed in 1976, and the authors are very enthusiastic about simulation gaming and/or use of simulations on computer technology as a vehicle to deliver the learning.

The authors of this article clarified the differences between the terms simulation games, role-playing games, and simulate role playing, and wanted to indicate that using simulation was not just an experience other than real-life. They were specific in spelling out the definitions of games and the restrictions that defined role-playing, as well a pointing out 'artificiality' as part of the simulation game environment. They pointed out a scenario used by a TV series (Mission Impossible) where the villains are convinced they are in an environment or talking to a real person versus an impersonator role-player.

This article also explained various terminologies synonymous with games and role-playing such as: 1) rules, 2) rituals, 3) boundaries, and 4) goals. Any simulator gaming situation in an educational setting should incorporate these aspects into the game to provide parameters to the learner so they know what to expect (generally) or what not to expect (surprise elements). Additionally student 'latitude' should be built into the simulation to encourage creative thinking, out-of-the-box solutions, and experimentation.

What also affects these elements above is the amount of artificiality of the simulation, the very nature of the activity, and the degree of learner participation based on the latitude allowed by the technique itself. The goals or objectives of the experience should end with meaningful questions and discussions to reach closure for the exercise and improve communications between the learners and the facilitator based on the learning objectives of the exercise.

Citations / Bibliography

Peters, W., Rogers, V., Dettre, J., Heger, H., Santoro, D. (1973), Individuality, individual differences, and computer simulation, *NASSP Bulletin, 57,* 43-49.

Command Post of the Future: Successful Transition of A Science and Technology Initiative to a Program of Record

This is a fascinating article about how an idea was moved from a virtual thought and plan to a software based workspace tool to support military cross-functional planning and execution of interoperability of the Army Battle Command System (ABCS) and enables the Army to work symbiotically with other DoD military services (Joint Forces). The sharing of intelligence between the various military services in a battle arena is vital to the successful operations of the military in a war zone, as well as in practice environments that provide the ability of collaboration and coordination between the elements. The authors noted that information dominance is vital to the success of any operation, as well as what makes the ability of these CPOF (Command Post of the Future) systems provide the warfighting commander (leader) situational awareness for synchronous execution of battle plans.

The article provides a history of the program, broken into four distinct phases. Phase I was the planning stage where the program investigated rich display technology, learning technologies, inference engines, and artificial intelligence and started around 1990 (early planning stages). To aid in the planning SME's worked with technology experts to create 'decision-support' exercises (simulation gaming) to bring a commonality within the community and atmosphere where technology and operations would be married to expertise in the planning of the CPOF.

In the fall of 2003, CPOF was introduced to the commander of the Army and the CPOF was introduced to the real-life battle theatre in Iraq. This operation was successful and DARPA and the Department of the Army (DoD) transitioned the program into every-day operations and established a collaboration for creating a more intuitive interface. There were major technological issues still unresolved and this teaming effort was meant to solve the operational and hardware procurement and technological research limitations.

The current ongoing efforts are related to modeling and simulation to enable the system to be 'theatre-wide' in a war arena with three challenges to overcome. The first was new technologies and data management strategies needed to be modeled against the current and future architecture (hardware and software capabilities) enabling scalability – can this system be used world-wide for all in-field units? The second issue is systems stability – also related to hardware and software capability, including server and satellite functionality and availability, as well as bandwidth use and availability. The third issue is Army Battle Command System (ABCS) interoperability – again related to a user community that allows user capability in real time, in a continuous feedback loop.

Since 2003, the increased users of the military for this CPOF (Command Post of the Future) systems has provided warfighting commanders increasingly sophisticated tools to plan, operate, and sustain action in the field through modeling and simulation technologies. What is truly interesting about this program is that experimentation in-theatre, spiral development, and development for future capabilities are done simultaneously and includes project management tools, testing, evaluation, risk exposure analysis, mitigation factors, and valuations of risk (acceptable or not acceptable) allows the warfighting commander to make instant decisions. The SME's (who were mostly retired military officers with experience in the field or battle arena) use the testing end of the system to model situations and recommend technology shifts or changes based on various modeling of simulations in the lab as well as the field.

Citations / Bibliography

Greene, H., Stotts, L., Paterson, R., & Greenberg, J. (2010, January). Command post of the future: successful transition of a science and technology initiative to a program of record. *Defense Acquisition Review Journal*, 17(1), 3-26.

Learning By Doing, Clark Aldrich

Aligning the Right Instructional Solution for the Right Problem

This appendix could be the poster child for 'lessons learned' in historic training to become the baseline for revising instructional techniques. I liked the author's attempt at humor related to 'skimming' over the materials. The suggested bulleted lists should be part of the plan when implementing any training program within a corporate setting, as well as within an educational setting, regardless of the material. The listing for the electronic/technical content is not only important for content, but from the 'back-end' perspective of what could happen if X goes wrong, and what Y solution would need to be put into place. The graphic on page 286 actually looks like an Adobe Connect screen from the facilitator's viewpoint.

I'm assuming that the definition the author is using for 'accord' is simply how well does everything work together, fit together, and interact between elements. The two graphics with Tier One and Two-Tiered End-Learners was interesting, but the author didn't provide enough text to fully describe the idea he was trying to illustrate in these graphics.

Citations/Bibliography

Aldrich, C. (2005). Appendix I, Aligning the right instructional solution for the right problem. *Learning by Doing.* (pp. 281-292). San Francisco, CA: John Wiley & Sons, Inc.

Authoring Learning Objects for Web-Based Intelligent Tutoring Systems

This article is related to education and competency-based course in Mexican schools for technical students in high school. As in the United States where most states have Standards or Standards of Learning (SOL) for pedagogical based education between kindergarten and high school, Mexico also has a standardized 'norm' for competency-based education. The norms are standardized to ensure a convenience measurement for planning, evaluating, and organizing the courses, and the conference presenters (authors) evaluate an authoring tool that is web-based to assist the teacher/trainer to develop three main components to the learning: 1) edit learning objects to create speedy 'web-based' class applications, 2) a visual player for displaying objects in an interface, and 3) a tutoring module to allow adding new features to the program relative to the learning object.

Whereas most understand CBT to stand for Computer Based Training, the authors of this paper note their definition as Competency Based Teaching. The components of this computer technology include user interfaces (instructor and student), a business model (using SCORM)[6] integrated with the course materials, and the data access element, which includes filters from HTML files, files (database) that interact together to create a program in which teachers can create their own training package for simulated training for the web. As the players use the tutorials as part of the interactive training package, they will open HTML files that give them baseline information, view course content, and then click on decision trees to lead them to the learning or interactivity module they need to achieve or complete.

This package was tested with college students in vocational technical training courses (Heat Transfer, Digital Systems, Mechanical design, etc.), and received a positive response (90% positive) from

---

[6] *SCORM is a set of technical standards, which specify how e-learning software should be built. It is the de facto industry standard for e-learning interoperability.*

assessments on the use of and effectiveness of the learning tool.

Providing instructors or facilitators the opportunities to create training packages via a software web-based tool to add value to the standards of learning increases user effectiveness and learning.

Citations / Bibliography

Zatarain-Cabada, R., Barron-Estrada, L., Zepeda-Sanchez, L., & Vega-Juarez, F. (2007). Authoring learning objects for the web-based intelligent tutoring systems. *Proceedings of the Advances in web-based learning – ICWL 2007, 6th international conference* (pp. 67-77). Edinburgh, UK: Springer.

Learning By Doing, Clark Aldrich
E-Learning Architecture Considerations Today

This appendix discusses the back-end pieces of computer based training which is identified here as a learning management system, which takes the elements of the content (community, multi-cast, content authoring, custom content, curriculum, administration, records (database)) and merge that with the considerations of firewalls, CBT, online or in-house elemental considerations. The author also touched base on whether the authoring tools should be PowerPoint or Flash based, but doesn't provide any other of the dozens, if not hundreds of e-learning programs that are available.

One element that is touched upon is the cost of such systems – often several tens of thousands of dollars for finished products, equating to between $12-$50 per user. This is symptomatic of the training product industry – the last company I was employed by was charged $12 per user license for an ethics training program for approximately 4,500 employees over the entire corporate entity (do the math - $540,000 annually for a ethics training program that probably cost about $50,000 to create; and they sell it to multiple companies – not just one.)

The author does touch base on elements the users need and should expect to easily manipulate the training modules to reach the end of the lesson. He also 'finishes' the experience content graphic by noting the experience should include various elements of paper, overheads, CD-ROM, internet portals, web applications (servers), Java Script, CSS, HTML, XML, and XSLT programming, should be wireless (capability), as well as have mail, a calendar, and a reporting tool for the learner's results (tied to the database itself).

Putting together an e-learning experience is a huge project and simply can't be achieved easily by one person – it requires a crew of experts in the various front-end and back-end design, programming, and user (customer) service end-product.

Citations/Bibliography

Aldrich, C. (2005). Appendix II, E-Learning architecture considerations today. *Learning by Doing.* (pp. 292-300). San Francisco, CA: John Wiley & Sons, Inc.

Learning By Doing, Clark Aldrich
Traditional Corporate Simulation Vendors

This appendix provides a quick overview of a list of game simulations that assist vendors in providing vertical and horizontal skills learning with branching stories, interactive spreadsheets, and virtual labs. Additionally a graph noted what market the various games and vendors target for the type of skill sets these games and simulations offer for training.

Citations/Bibliography

Aldrich, C. (2005). Appendix III: traditional corporate simulation vendors. *Learning by Doing.* (pp. 292-300). San Francisco, CA: John Wiley & Sons, Inc.

Resources for Simulation and Gaming Theory:

www.gametheory.net/lectures/field.pl

(Reference list viable as of 2010)

IndustryMasters
www.industrymasters.com
IndustryMasters browser-based business simulation with more than 200 industries grouped into 16 industry sectors: Aerospace, Automotive, Beverages, Energy, Cosmetics, Appliances, Electronics, Recreation, Agriculture, Processed Food ,Staple Food, Machinery, Metal, Pharma, Wood & Paper,Textile. IndustryMasters simulates all aspects of management: from Strategy, Investment and Finance to Product Pricing, Marketing, Quality, R&D, HR and Ecology.
You take the role of an entrepreneur and compete live against players from around the globe for market share, profit and shareholder value.

Lemonade Stand on the iPhone iPod
www.ustream.tv/recorded/1445088
Lemonade Stand on the iPhone iPod
Tony Vincent shares some of his favorite iPod touch and iPhone apps for education. There's also audience participation. Lemonade Stand is an App that he demos at the beginning of this UStream presentation

Bossingame - Business Game
www.bossingame.com/index.php?lang=en
Dare yourself and rock this online Business Game!
Manage your own virtual company, compete against

international players and become famous with your management skills!

The Science of Spore--The
http://tinyurl.com/79vdw4
The Science of Spore--The "Evolution" of Gaming
Spore encompasses five stages of development: cell, creature, tribe, civilization and space. There are some potent differences, however, between evolution as it actually operates and Spore's animated version of events. For one, in the "cell" and "creature" stages of the game, organisms win "DNA points" when they achieve certain goals.

Titan : Business Simulation
http://titan.ja.org/
Titan : Business Simulation
Test your skills running a business in this ultimate business simulation! As CEO, you will match wits in the competitive, technologically advanced industry of the Holo-Generator
Set in the year 2035, JA Titan creates a world in which players are CEOs of their own companies. Originally conceived in the 1980s as the Management and Economic Simulation Exercise, or MESE, JA Titan is a widely recognized business simulation for high school students.
During game play, students must run a manufacturing company and master six key business decisions: price of product, production levels, marketing expenses, research and development costs, capital investment level, and charitable giving. Various corporate assistants "help" the player through each phase, or "quarter," of game play.

ElectroCity
http://electrocity.co.nz/
ElectroCity is an online computer game that lets players manage their own virtual towns and cities.
It's great fun to play and also teaches players all about energy, sustainability and environmental management in New Zealand. Just think up a city name and declare yourself Mayor.
If you're a school teacher, you need to register so your students' cities are eligible for school prizes.

Learning by Simulations
www.vias.org/simulations/
Simulations play a central role in learning by doing, since the understanding of concepts and fundamental ideas is closely related to being able to experiment with a topic or a particular aspect of it.
Learning by Simulations has been developed to support both teachers and students in the process of knowledge transfer and knowledge acquisition. It currently contains about 40 simulations dealing with mathematical, phyiscal, chemical, or computer science problems. Most of the simulations are available both in English and German language.

Discover! Simulations ... Science
www.eduplace.com/kids/hmsc/content/simulation/
Discover! Simulations ... Science
An IMPRESSIVE collection from Houghton Mifflin Science

The Shodor Foundation
www.shodor.org/
"The Shodor Foundation, a nonprofit education and research corporation, is "dedicated to the advancement of science and math education, specifically through the use of modeling and simulation technologies." Shodor recognized that professional computational science tools, especially graphics and animations, could be adapted for classroom use.
The foundation's Web site offers access to a repertoire of software and provides value-added aids, such as curriculum materials for students, sorted by grade and subject, for students, teachers, and parents."

Hotel and Tourism Workplace Simulator
http://project.shtm.polyu.edu.hk/new-index.html
Hotel and Tourism Workplace Simulator .. from the Hong Kong Polytechnic University

Idaho Bioterrorism (Second Life)
http://irhbt.typepad.com/play2train/
Play2Train - Idaho Bioterrorism Awareness and Preparedness

Program
Play2Train is a virtual training space in SecondLife designed to support Strategic National Stockpile (SNS), Simple Triage Rapid Transportation (START), Risk Communication and Incident Command System (ICS) Training.
This virtual environment spreads over two islands Asterix and Obelix (65536 x 2 sq. meters), with one island dedicated to a virtual town and the other a virtual hospital. The design of this virtual environment is influenced by dioramas frequently used by emergency services to support their tabletop exercises.

Hydro Hijinks Diplomacy Game (Second Life)
www.youtube.com/watch?v=JS2JT9IV3CM
Hydro Hijinks Diplomacy Game
Updated (as of 03/26) walkthrough of an award-winning diplomacy game created in Second Life, by the students of IS195 at Montgomery College, Rockville Maryland.

Hydro Hijinks Diplomacy Game (Second Life)
www.youtube.com/watch?v=JS2JT9IV3CM
Hydro Hijinks Diplomacy Game
Updated (as of 03/26) walkthrough of an award-winning diplomacy game created in Second Life, by the students of IS195 at Montgomery College, Rockville Maryland.

UC Davis' Virtual Hallucinations (Second Life)
www.ucdmc.ucdavis.edu/ais/virtualhallucinations/
UC Davis' Virtual Hallucinations (Second Life) Sec.Life Landmark / SLurl

The Heart Murmur Sim (Second Life)
http://sl.nmc.org/2006/09/25/jeremy-kemp/
The Heart Murmur Sim
Jeremy Kemp (Jeremy Kabumpo in SL) looks over his Heart Murmur Simulation site, located in the Waterhead region of Second Life. Jeremy provided a quick walk through tour of his Heart Murmur simulation, which features use of special audio features to provide the needed sounds to simulate cardiac auscultation.

NationStates
www.nationstates.net/
NationStates is a free nation simulation game. Build a nation and run it according to your own warped political ideals. Create a Utopian paradise for society's less fortunate or a totalitarian corporate police state. Care for your people or deliberately oppress them. Join the United Nations or remain a rogue state. It's really up to you.

Google Earth Flight Simulator
www.sajaforum.org/2007/09/web-google-eart.html
Google Earth Flight Simulator
You can choose to fly one of two planes. The F16 is almost impossible to control for novices, so the SR22 propeller plane is the way to go (and offers better sightseeing).
You can choose to start from your current position on G.E., or you can choose from several airports around the world, including the Kathmandu one.

aVataR@School project
www.avataratschool.eu/mod/resource/view.php?id=83
The overall project goal is to use virtual role plays to find a new way for conflict resolutions with a playful and cooperative approach. The project's goals are to establish virtual role plays in which pupils and teachers try strategies for conflict resolution by means of the School Peer Mediation approach. Each virtual role plays will take plave in a popular 3D online digital world: SecondLife (www.secondlife.com). Each role plays a scenario represents a typical conflict in school (e.g. social exclusion, bullying or violence). In each scenario players will try to find common solutions in a cooperative and collaborative way.

Train Spotting Simulator
www.ratbike.org/tspotsim/
Microtoss Train Spotting Simulator brings the power and excitement of one of the world's most favorite hobbies to your PC, placing you in the role of a trainspotter with unprecedented realism, exciting real-world challenges, and the tools to recreate almost any trainspotting experience in the world.

The Classroom Sim : Simulation Discipline Strategies
http://ahaprocess.com/store/Sims.html
The Classroom Sim can help you refine your discipline skills before you ever set foot in the classroom. You simply play the computer game by making classroom decisions, enforcing and modifying rules, and responding to events initiated by students, parents, and administrators. At the end of each quarter you will receive feedback on how your decisions might affect the happiness, behavior, and academic progress of your students. Set includes Simulation Software Activation and Companion Edition Book: Working with Students: Discipline Strategies for the 21st Century; Simulation Companion Edition

Google Maps Flight Simulator
www.isoma.net/games/goggles.html
Google Maps Flight Simulator
Fly a small model aeroplane anywhere ... but using Google maps .. so the scenary is real!

Free Simulation Games at Windows Marketplace
http://tinyurl.com/gdrj2
Free Education Simulation Games at Windows Marketplace Select from hundreds of free (and commercial) games and demos, plus patches to improve the performance of games you already own.

Download Full (Old) Games for free
www.download-full-games.com/pc/educational/index.html
Download Full Games : Free Simulations (over 300). Games are free to download ... this collection is of 'old favourites' .. in fact 'classics' .. that have been 'retired' but still useful for teaching and learning.

PeaceMaker
www.etc.cmu.edu/projects/peacemaker/TheGame.htm
PeaceMaker is a one-player game in which the player can choose to take the role of either the Israeli Prime Minister or the Palestinian President. The player must react to in-game events, from diplomatic negotiations to military attacks, and interact with eight other political leaders and social groups in order to

establish a stable resolution to the conflict before his or her term in office ends.
Real-time and Location-Based Events. Videos and pictures from a library of real-time news events are interjected into gameplay. Relevant events are presented on a high-resolution map of Israel, the West Bank, and the Gaza Strip.

Simulations from Persuasive Games
www.persuasivegames.com/games/
Simulations at Persuasive Games
This company produces several simulations that would be useful in a number of different curriculum areas
Disaffected! - a videogame parody of the Kinko's copy store, a source of frustration from its patrons. Disaffected! puts the player in the role of employees forced to service customers under the particular incompetences common to a Kinko's store.
Airport Insecurity - a game about inconvenience and the tradeoffs between security and rights in American airports.
Stone City – Cold Stone Creamery, Inc. - Cold Stone commissioned an employee training game to focus on the issue portion sizes and their relationship to profitability.

Informatist Guide
www.informatistguide.jumbahost.com/index.php
Guide for Informatist.
Informatist is a free, business simulation game, which features joint stock companies and a fluctuating stock market.
It's free to play, and is regularly updated.

Bath time with Archimedes : Handling Data
http://tinyurl.com/qbf2s
Bath time with Archimedes : Handling Data
Key Stages 2 and 3: Age range 10 - 14
This simulation involves changing variables by selecting the strength of the water flow into the bath, turning the tap on or off, putting the plug in and out, and telling Archimedes to get in and out of the bath.

Car Seat belt crash simulator
www.thinkseatbelts.co.uk/
Car Seat belt crash simulator

Gibbity : Simulations : Reviews
www.gibbity.com/content/world/simulation/0/all/8/0
Gibbity : Simulations : Reviews
Gibbity is a people-powered, game discovery engine. As a participant, you can either explore the current game listings and review stuff you find, or you could contribute games that aren't there yet and review those.
web 2.0

Lemonade Stand
www.primarygames.com/socstudies/lemonade/start.htm
Lemonade Stand
Welcome to Lemonade Stand! Your goal in this game will be to make as much money as you can within 30 days. To do this, you've decided to open your own business -- a Lemonade Stand! You'll have complete control over almost every part of your business, including pricing, quality control, inventory control, and purchasing supplies. You'll also have to deal with the weather, which can be unpredictable.

Cellular Automata
http://grant.robinson.name/projects/cellularAutomata/
Cellular Automata
A simulation of cell behaviour based on four simple rules.
I'm fascinated by how a seemingly complex organic system can be created from such a simple set of rules. Make sure you try creating your own initial setup to see how it survives.

llor
http://llor.nu/
The object of the game is to become the player with the highest net worth. There is one primary way of doing this: buying hotels and waiting for other players to land on them, paying you rent.

Informatist
www.informatist.net/
Open economics game/simulation. Players compete in order to dominate market and achieve best financial results. The game is open - anyone can play it without any cost.
No special software required - web browser is enough.
Online massive multiplayer economics game

Food Force
www.food-force.com/
"Food Force" is a free online game from the United Nations World Food Program that sends children ages 8 to 13 on six realistic aid missions.
Food Force serves as a classroom tool for teaching about hunger.
From the United Nations World Food Programme (WFP), the world? largest humanitarian agency, Food Force is an educational video game telling the story of a hunger crisis on the fictitious island of Sheylan.
Comprised of 6 mini-games or ?issions? the game takes young players from an initial crisis assessment through to delivery and distribution of food aid, with each sequential mission addressing a particular aspect of this challenging process.
The game has wide cross-curricular appeal (geography, social studies, health, etc.) and can strengthen strategic thinking and decision-making skills. It is an ideal lesson follow-up or homework activity.
Teachers are encouraged to download the game and install it on school computers or burn it onto a CD and make as many copies as required.

Power Politics 3
www.powerpolitics.us/
Power Politics 3 : USA Presidential Campaign Simulator

Environment Simulation
www.kineticcity.com/controlcar/activity.php?act=4&virus=flossil
Environment Simulation
Until recently, most of the environments on Earth stayed pretty much the same for hundreds or even thousands of years. But now, humans can change an environment practically overnight. Just think what a bulldozer can do to a two-thousand-year-old forest! In this Mind Game, you?l see how big changes to the environment can affect the animals that live there.
In this game, you can control how much pollution lands on the trees. Just click on the slider and drag it toward "More Pollution" (orange) or "Less Pollution" (green). Then sit back and watch what happens to the bugs!

Chemistry Simulations
http://chemcollective.org/applets/
Chemistry Simulations
Virtual Chemistry Laboratory | Acclimatization on Mt. Everest | Stoichiometry | Periodic Table | Internal Combustion Engine Simulator | Why Things Have Color | Equilibrium | Spectroscopic Simulator | Statistical Mechanical Simulator |

Strombolian Eruption Simulation
http://volcano.und.nodak.edu/vwdocs/kids/fun/volcano/volcano.html
Strombolian Eruption Simulation (Volcanoe)

Extreme Farm Simulation
www.frozenden.x3fusion.com/flash/farmsim.html
Extreme Farm Simulation ;-)

Zoo Tycoon
www.microsoft.com/games/pc/zootycoon.aspx
In Zoo Tycoon, you'll be challenged to build the most healthy and vibrant zoo possible. With an easy to learn interface, you can begin planning your strategy and building your ultimate zoo the moment you start the game.
Plan poorly, and those lions, tigers, and bears may find a new found interest in you! Zoo Tycoon - enjoy the fun and challenge of building and managing the ultimate zoo.
Zoo Tycoon Trial Version .. free download 27MB
zoo | animal | simulation |

Virtual Worlds at Biz/Ed
www.bized.ac.uk/virtual/home.htm
Virtual Worlds at Biz/Ed
Virtual Economy : The model is based around No.11 Downing St. - the Chancellor's house and office. Here's your chance to run the economy better than the Chancellor.
Virtual Developing Country : Find out more about development economics through our Zambia case study.
Virtual Bank : What do banks and central banks do? Take a trip down to our Virtual Bank to find out.
Virtual Learning Arcade : Do you want to have a go at determining a house price? Run this and other simulations.
Virtual Factory : find out about everything from production to

accounts.
Virtual Farm : Can you run the family farm for ten years and make a profit? What could possibly go wrong?

Evolution Lab
www.biologyinmotion.com/evol/index.html
Evolution Lab ... evolution simulation

The Quest for Independence
www.ottersurf.com/quest/
The Quest for Independence
An interactive simulation that enables kids to spend money, get a job -- or suffer the consequences of spending all their money without getting a job!

Sports simulations
www.vcaa.vic.edu.au/prep10/csf/support/sampleunits/Sports_simulations.pdf
Sports simulations : MATHEMATICS Levels 5 and 6
In Sports simulations students simulate well-known sports using dice and compare their results with real data from the games played on sports fields.
Students also use simulations to investigate the range of winning-run lengths for teams that are evenly matched or otherwise.

Sports Simulations List on Google
http://directory.google.com/Top/Sports/Fantasy/Simulations/
Sports Simulations List on Google

Simulation Sports Leagues
www.playasport.com/index.html
Simulation Sports Leagues
Playasport users can participate in one of many simulation sports games, including baseball, basketball, football, hockey, and soccer.
Additionally we have tennis, figure skating, golf, and racing games that let you manage your own player through a season of events.
Playasport is a free sports simulation site, with daily results and rankings.

Learning Simulations
www.learnativity.com/simulations.html
Learning Simulations
Technology and more wide-spread understanding that people learn best by doing shines a bright light on new, more simulation-focused products and services. Much of this work is rooted in experiential learning but now with a techno-twist.
Overview of learning simulations | Any good books and articles about Simulations? | Organizations that focus on this stuff? | Who's building simulation tools? |

Real Lives : Simulation
www.educationalsimulations.com/products.html
Educational Simulations presents Real Lives 2004, the life simulation that gives you the opportunity to learn how people really live in other countries.
You might be born anyone, anywhere on Earth. You might die as an infant, you might make it to old age. You might be able to marry the person of your dreams, and have a rewarding job, or you could be stuck in poverty. Be born, live an exciting life, and die. Then do it again. And again. Learn about the world as you live your Real Lives around the world, one life-altering decision at a time.
simulation

Coffee Tycoon
www.bigfishgames.com/downloads/coffeetycoon/index.html
Coffee Tycoon lets gamers build a coffee empire. Starting fresh with one store, players customize their coffee business by giving it a name and choosing a logo and store design. From there, they'll choose a city to start their coffee empire, maybe New York or L.A., or if they're really daring, the coffee capital of the world: Seattle!
FREE downloadable **trial** version (12 MB)

Diner Dash
www.bigfishgames.com/downloads/dinerdash/
Diner Dash
Diner Dash Diner Dash blends the best in fast paced-action puzzles with a build-your-restaurant-empire theme that encourages players to serve their way from a two-table diner to the top of the restaurant ladder - starting with a run-of-the-mill

greasy spoon and ending in a dream restaurant that will take your breath away.
FREE trial version (10.4 MB)

FlightGear: open-source, multi-platform flight simulator.
www.flightgear.org/
FlightGear : an open-source, multi-platform flight simulator. The goal of the FlightGear project is to create a sophisticated flight simulator framework for use in research or academic environments, for the development and pursuit of other interesting flight simulation ideas, and as an end-user application.
We are developing a sophisticated, open simulation framework that can be expanded and improved upon by anyone interested in contributing.

ABOUT THE AUTHOR

Dawn D. Boyer, Ph.D. completed her Doctor of Philosophy in Education (Occupational & Technical Studies, with a concentration in Training & Development in Human Resources) from Old Dominion University in Norfolk, VA in 2013. Her dissertation is entitled, 'Competencies of Human Resources Practitioners within the Government Contracting Industry,' which identified unique KSAs for Human Resources Managers working for federal level government contracting companies. This groundbreaking research is the impetus upon her textbook guide for Human Resources Professionals in Government Contracting, currently in the works.

She has been an entrepreneur and business owner for 14+ years, currently in her consulting firm, D. Boyer Consulting, based in Richmond (Henrico County), VA, and servicing clients internationally. Her background experience is 24+ years in the Human Resources field, of which 11 years are within the federal defense contracting industry.

Dr. Boyer's experience in federal (defense) contracting as a Human Resources Director or Senior Manager has provided her insight, experience, practice, and capabilities to perform within this industry, as well as instruct others to abilities needed in middle-management or executive human resource roles.

Dr. Boyer currently works with job and new career seekers to write Search Engine Optimized resumes for increased visibility to recruiters – getting the candidates past the recruiting 'firewall' and interviewed for faster hires and job placement. Her tech-based knowledge of how the ATS software systems work help job seekers in structuring a resume for recruiters' Boolean search queries. Her SEO coding within resume is so unique, no other resume writers offer this service.

She additionally assists academics and writers publish their works or manuscripts as a third-party publisher – DBC Publishing. She also assists business owners develop their brand and marketing plans within social media marketing, planning, and management.

She is the author of over 145 books on the topics of genealogy, family lineage, women and gender studies, business and career search practice, quotes for self-improvement and motivation (2,000+ /3,000+ series), and her 'Interview with an Artist' series (three artists in the series to date). All of her books are listed on her Amazon author's page at:

https://www.amazon.com/author/dawnboyer.

Dr. Boyer has been a member of LinkedIn since 2004 (a few months after beta version released) and has developed a rich profile for consistent and constant communications to ~12,600+ connections. Her clients call her 'The Queen of LinkedIn.'

She may be reached via her business website:

http://DBoyerConsulting.com

or by email:

Dawn.Boyer@DBoyerConsulting.com

CURRICULUM VITAE

DAWN D. BOYER, Ph.D.

B.F.A., M.Ad.Ed., CDR, CIR, LSS - Green Belt, Virginia Beach, VA

- 24+ years, HR, Employee Relations, Recruiting, Training, Development, Presentations, Benefits/Compensation, Analysis/Auditing, and Employment Law/ Practices
- 13+ years, Entrepreneur, Business Owner, Business Partner
- 11+ years, Federal Defense Contractors (SBA 8(a), HUB Zone, Service Disabled Veteran Owned Business, Woman Owned, and Alaskan Native Corporation [ANC])
- 11+ years, Federal / Government Contracts Employment Issues and Laws
- 8+ years, Teaching, Training and Curriculum Development in business, information technology, and Human Resources in proprietary and public educational institutions
- 7+ years, Contracts Negotiations and Insurance Benefits Administration
- 3+ years, Graduate Teaching Assistant (GTA) for Undergraduate Studies

EMPLOYMENT HISTORY

08/10 - present, Resume Writing Subject Matter Expert, Social Media Management Consultant, Editing & Publishing (dba DBC Publishing), D. Boyer Consulting, Virginia Beach and Richmond, VA

12/15 – 06/16, Adjunct Professor, Art Institute of Virginia Beach, VA

06/15 – present, Reviewer/Editor, Academic Publications

08/09 – 12/12, Adjunct Instructor & Doctoral Graduate Teaching Assistant, Old Dominion University, Norfolk, VA

06/07 – 09/17, Vice President / HR Director, Business Development, and Social Media Manager
Monster Clean, Carpet, Oriental Rug & Upholstery Cleaning, Virginia Beach, VA

11/07 – 03/09, Director, Human Resources & Ethics Compliance
Chenega Advanced Solutions & Engineering, LLC, Norfolk, VA

05/05 – 11/07, Senior Corporate Recruiting Manager, Zel Technologies, LLC (ZelTech), Hampton, VA

01/03 – 04/05, Human Resources Manager (Corporate Specialist), AMSEC LLC (Corp HQ's) (a LLC between SAIC & Northrop Grumman Newport News Shipbuilding), Virginia Beach, VA (Corporate HQ's), (Subsidiary companies: Egan McAllister & Associates (EMA), PMI, M. Rosenblatt & Son, Inc., etc.)

03/01 – 01/03, AMSEC Human Resources Manager, LLC (IMEG / SETS Group)

07/95 – 01/01, Human Resources Manager, Norfolk Warehouse Mgmt. / The Taylor Cos., Norfolk, VA

12/94 - 07/95, Human Resources Creative Generalist, Metro Information Services, Inc., Va. Beach, VA

FORMAL EDUCATION

Doctor of Philosophy (PhD), **Old Dominion University**, Norfolk, VA; *Occupational and Technical Studies (Science, Technology, Engineering & Math in Professional Studies (STEMPS); concentration in Training & Development in Human Resources; GPA: 3.65*

Masters Degree in Education, Virginia Commonwealth University, Richmond, VA (1989), Adult Education - Human Resources, Training & Development, Personnel, and Staffing; GPA: 3.67

Bachelors Degree in Fine Art, Advertising, and Graphic Illustration, Radford University, Radford, VA (1983); Graphic Advertising & Illustration, Fine Art, and Art History; GPA: 3.25

Follow the Author on Social Media Platforms

D. Boyer Consulting

DBoyerConsulting.com

Join her 12,600+ connections on LinkedIn:

www.linkedin.com/in/DawnBoyer

Amazon Author Page:

www.amazon.com/author/dawnboyer

Review Author's books:

www.shelfari.com/DawnDeniseBoyer

Twitter at:

www.Twitter.com/Dawn_Boyer

YouTube Channel:

www.youtube.com/user/DawnDeniseBoyer

Interested in publishing your own academic essays, projects, or books? Contact the author for publishing project estimates, consulting, and assistance:

Dawn.Boyer@me.com
www.DBoyerConsulting.com

ABOUT THE BOOK

This book outlines and describes a Modeling and Simulation project completed in the 2010 class of Old Dominion Universities' Occupational and Technical Studies in Education class, Issues in Training, Modeling and Simulation class. The assignment was to create a Simulation Lesson Design.

The book showcases the assignment (proposal) for an instructional lesson that utilized simulation in support of a specific training or educational goal or objective. Using lectures in the classroom, assigned readings, and literature reviews, the following lesson plan was developed as the final project in the class. Additionally, this book includes annotations and resources to gain more in-depth understanding of the principal and the project.

www.ingramcontent.com/pod-product-compliance
Lightning Source LLC
Chambersburg PA
CBHW060837050426
42453CB00008B/730